200 Lessons From My Early 20's

Hailto

Copyright © 2023 Hailto

All rights reserved.

ISBN: 9798872182887

*Dedicated to all my readers,
whose unwavering support became my
pillar of strength during challenging times*

This one's for you

CONTENTS

Introduction   i

Part 1   1
Friendships

Part 2   56
Love

Part 3   131
Life

INTRODUCTION

Your 20's is the time to become financially savvy, identify true friendships, establish independence, and understand what you truly want out of a romantic relationship.
Your 20's is the time to uncover your true self.

"200 Lessons From My Early 20's" takes you through my experiences in my early 20's on friendships, love, and life. At the time of writing this book, I am 23 years old. And yes, while that is a young age to learn such lessons, I am happy for the experiences in my life to allow me to pass them down to my readers.

Whether you are entering, navigating, or leaving your 20's, there is always an opportunity for self-discovery and growth. Embracing the lessons from challenging experiences is essential for evolving into the best version of yourself.

The best revenge is becoming the best version of yourself.
- Hailto

Part 1

Friendships

Lesson 1

Remember who checks on you
When you're a little too quiet

Those are your people

Lesson 2

Never trust people with too many friends
All they do is share your problems
With other people

Oh, and gossip about you, too

Lesson 3

Real friends will never
Use your vulnerabilities
Against you

Lesson 4

Be aware of how a friend
Treats their significant other

If they can cheat on them
They can cheat you, too

Lesson 5

Be wary of the ones who come into your life
Only when they need something from you

Lesson 6

If they don't
Talk to you
Reach out to you
Make plans with you
Check how you're doing
Unless you initiate it

They don't like you

Lesson 7

Stay away from the girls who crave
Male validation
Because
They will drop you instantly
For any guy

Lesson 8

Surround yourself with friends
Who inspire you to become
A better version of yourself

Negative energy can
Bleed into your space
And make you a
Negative person

Lesson 9

Don't hold onto toxic friendships
Just because
You're afraid to make new friends

Lesson 10

You can have

Party friends
Close friends
Work friends
Gym friends
Online friends
Family friends
Hobby friends
Travel friends

Lesson 11

If they care about you
Being honest about how you feel
Won't scare them away

Lesson 12

The way someone acts
In a room full of people
They are trying to impress
Will tell you more than enough about them

Lesson 13

Real friends will

Tell you the truth
Keep you accountable
Reach out to you
Be a shoulder to cry on
Lift you up when you're down
Defend you in front of others

Lesson 14

You are who you surround yourself with
And if you don't like your top 5 friends

Change them

Lesson 15

Do you feel like you are
Walking on eggshells
Everytime you're around them?

Then they're not for you

Lesson 16

Keep the same expectations
For your friendships
As you would
For your relationships

Lesson 17

A friend who reaches out
Only between their romantic relationships
Is not a friend

Lesson 18

Are you energized
Or drained
After hanging out with someone?

Lesson 19

Most friends are not
Everything friends

That's what best friends are for

Lesson 20

Friendship should be mutual
They should want to be your friend
As much as you want to be
Their friend

Lesson 21

Always support your friends
In things that they are
Passionate and care about

Be there for them
Just like they are for you

Lesson 22

Befriend people off of
Compatibility
Not proximity

Lesson 23

There is a difference between
Becoming friends
And
Making friends

One is natural
The other is forced

Lesson 24

A friend should never
Raise their voice at you

Lesson 25

The older you get
The harder it becomes
To maintain friendships

But life goes on

Lesson 26

Friends who keep you accountable
And call you out on your B.S.
Actually care about you

Keep them close

Lesson 27

What might be ok for you
Might not be ok for your friend

Communication is key
Even in friendships

Lesson 28

Tell your friends you love them
< 3

Lesson 29

Don't let a man
Ruin your friendship

Lesson 30

Just because you haven't spoken to them
In a long time
Doesn't mean the friendship
Has disappeared

Give them a call

Lesson 31

A friend who is always making jokes
At your expense
Is not just joking

Lesson 32

A true friend is someone
Who can be happy for you
Without making it about themselves

Lesson 33

The length of a friendship
Does not correlate
With the quality of the friendship

Lesson 34

Sometimes friends grow apart
And that's ok

Lesson 35

You don't have to spend every second with someone
For that friendship to be meaningful

Lesson 36

Having a hard time making new friends?
Join an activity you enjoy
And find like-minded people there

Lesson 37

You can have a friendship
That feels more like a soulmate

There is comfort in knowing
You can talk about life
Without judgment

Lesson 38

You've grown apart if

You say you miss them
But never bother to call

You hold onto positive memories
But won't make new ones

You love them
But don't like them as much as before

Lesson 39

True friends can
Grow separately
Without growing apart

Lesson 40

Don't be surprised if
Friends who aren't doing better than you
Aren't happy for your success

Lesson 41

How to be a good friend:

Initiate plans
Be supporting
Call them
Be honest
Text them back
Be by their side
Never put boys above them
Include them
Comfort them
Love them

Lesson 42

I have lost a lot of friends
In my life
And I realized
True friends are the ones who will
Take accountability
Apologize
And change to be better

Lesson 43

Not having a lifelong best friend
Sucks but
Meeting new people
Who immediately accept you
For who you are
Is an even better feeling

Lesson 44

Having a strong female friendship
Will forever be more beautiful
Than any romantic relationship
I have encountered

Lesson 45

Signs you are a backup friend:

You always initiate contact
They have limited availability
You only get last second invites
They exclude you from plans
You feel unappreciated
They don't share anything intimate
You have a gut feeling

Trust your gut

Lesson 46

Make sure your friends
Can see their own beauty

Lesson 47

A good friend
Will know when
Your smile is disappearing
Your heart is breaking
Your soul is aching
Your spark is fading

And will try their best
To heal you through the pain

Lesson 48

Friendship breakups
Hurt way more than
Romantic breakups

Lesson 49

You need to let go of
Your high school friends

You can still be friends
But don't let those friendships
Stop you from making new ones

You cannot grow to your
Full potential
If you are constantly surrounded
By your teenage past

Lesson 50

You need to realize
When your friends are no longer
Serving you purpose

Some friends will keep us down
To boost their self-esteem

Just because they hang out with you
Doesn't mean they respect you

Lesson 51

Always support your friends
But
Don't let their bad habits
Rub off on you

Lesson 52

To my friends who
No longer wanted to be my friend
I'm sorry if I ever did you wrong
And wish you communicated with me
Instead of slowly and silently
Pushing me
Away

Lesson 53

Types of people I would
Never be friends with:

Girls who prefer male friendships
The one who gossips about a close friend
Those who maintain friendships with my ex

Someone who stays friends with someone
Who did me so wrong

Lesson 54

In my darkest hours
My friends were my lifeline
Pulling me from the depths of despair

Be grateful for your friends
And remember to thank them
For showing up

To my dearest friends
Thank you

Part 2

Love

Lesson 55

Relationships suck

You're scared you won't have one
And when you do
You're scared you'll lose it

Lesson 56

If they leave over something stupid
They weren't planning
To stay for the long run

Don't beat yourself up over it

Lesson 57

The loneliest you will ever be
Is feeling unseen in a relationship

Don't let comfort keep you somewhere
That isn't serving you anymore

Lesson 58

If you want to know what type of guy he is
Watch how he treats others
Who can offer nothing to him

Lesson 59

Easiest ways to kill a relationship:

Ignoring boundaries
Lying
Comparing to others
Refusing to compromise
Lack of communication
Disregarding your partner's needs
Being overly critical

Taking your partner for granted

Lesson 60

Attachment is not love

Lesson 61

You can't make someone understand
If it's beyond their understanding

Lesson 62

Don't confuse having boundaries
With being controlling

Lesson 63

It is a privilege to know you
It is a privilege to be with you
It is a privilege to love you
It is a privilege to be loved by you

Lesson 64

People are a reflection of
Who they surround themselves with

Lesson 65

A strong romantic relationship
Starts with a strong friendship

Lesson 66

Don't let someone have to
Tell you and show you
Multiple times
That they don't want you

Lesson 67

Commitment
Requires
Sacrifice

Lesson 68

Sometimes it's hard to let go of what's making you sad
Because at one point
It was the only thing that made you happy

Lesson 69

He's not going to like you more
If you try harder

Lesson 70

Do not listen to words
Only listen to actions

Lesson 71

They say a man will only change
For the woman he wants

WRONG

He will only change for himself
When he feels like it

Lesson 72

The right person will come to you
But
You need to put yourself out there
For the right person to find you

Lesson 73

Hearing is different than listening

Lesson 74

Love should feel like friendship on fire

Lesson 75

It's not about who you want to
Spend Friday night with
But
Who you want to
Spend all day Saturday with

Lesson 76

You don't need the love
That doesn't come to you freely

Lesson 77

People go
And how they left
Always stays

Lesson 78

If they are mistreating you
It is often a reflection of how they feel
About themselves

Lesson 79

Just because he changed your life
Doesn't mean he's meant to stay in your life forever

Lesson 80

It's never too late to leave

Lesson 81

Take responsibility for your own happiness
Instead of
Putting unrealistic expectations
On your partner

Lesson 82

Sometimes it's better to be ghosted
Than strung along

Lesson 83

Never dim your lights so some man can feel
Like his shine brighter

You are not too much

Lesson 84

What keeps love going?
Compromise

Lesson 85

If he wanted to, he would
Is awful advice
But
If he won't, someone else will
Is a better mindset

Lesson 86

He doesn't know you like a book
He can read the chapters
But unwritten pages hold the depth
Of your untold story

Make sure to communicate
Those unwritten pages to him

Lesson 87

Learn about your love languages
And your partner's
So you can love each other better

Lesson 88

May you attract a relationship
Where conversations feel like
Building bridges and not war zones

Lesson 89

Your frontal lobe fully develops
At age 25
And is responsible for
Thinking
Emotions
Judgment
Self-control
Memory

If a man is older than 25
And is still
Emotionally inept

LEAVE HIM SISTER!!!

Lesson 90

If he calls his ex crazy
Just know
He made her crazy

Lesson 91

Don't stay in a relationship
If it's not working
Even if you invested
1, 2, even 10 years into it

You have your whole life ahead of you

Lesson 92

At the end of the day

It's the person who
You run to without hesitation
No matter the distance

It's the person who
Knows when you are upset
Even when you try to hide it

It's the person who
Understands you
Even when you don't understand yourself

It's the person who
Gives you warmth
Even when your heart is cold

Lesson 93

It's ok for him to acknowledge
Someone else's beauty
As long as he acknowledges
You are the most beautiful of them all

Lesson 94

Alcohol won't help you forget him

It'll just help you remember him
With a hangover

Lesson 95

He isn't treating her any better
She just has a lower tolerance
Think of it like this:

Your capacity is a level 7
He is a level 4
His competence keeps him at a 4
No matter how hard he tries

His new girl, however, is also a level 4
She requires less of him
Making them more compatible

And you need someone who can meet you
At level 7
Not level 4

Lesson 96

We all have 'icks'
Don't let one ick be a dealbreaker

Lesson 97

Avoid the guy who sees
Putting you down as a joke
But
Putting him down as an insult

Lesson 98

Some awful things my ex said to me:

Why is it always me saying sorry?
You need to stop being sensitive
Should I remove you from my social media?
Are you going to send me a paragraph about
this in the morning?

And my favorite:
Just because I do something nice once
Doesn't mean I'm expected to do it again

Lesson 99

If you read the same book twice
It doesn't change the ending

And we all know
The sequel is never any better

Lesson 100

What he does after the breakup
Has nothing to do with you
But <u>everything</u> to do with himself

If he moves on quickly
He simply does not want to deal
With the feelings of heartbreak

Let him be and let him
Continue in that damaging cycle

He is insecure
And cannot be alone

Lesson 101

Just because you spend time together
Doesn't make it quality time

Do something you both enjoy
Equally

Lesson 102

Insecurity is not an insult
It's an emotion

Lesson 103

If you fight with your partner
DO NOT
Go to your friends and family

Once you resolve that fight
And move on
The sour taste is left in their mouth

Lesson 104

Don't date a guy
Who's Instagram following
Looks like he went to
An all-girls school

Lesson 105

If he sees
Spending time with you as a chore
And he'd rather play video games
With his friends on Saturday night

Let him play games with them
Every night

So you can find a guy
Who wants to spend every night with you

Lesson 106

If you have to chase it
It's not yours

Lesson 107

One of the boldest things
You could ever do
Is love someone

When you open yourself to love
You open yourself to be hurt

Lesson 108

You can break something in two seconds
But it can take a lifetime to fix it

Be gentle with your partner

Lesson 109

The most challenging relationship
Is the healthy one after a toxic one

Keep your heart open to love
And love will find you

Lesson 110

Don't be regretful of a bad relationship
It was a learning lesson

Love is a privilege

Lesson 111

He made fun of my body
He called me the b word
He manipulated me
He disliked my culture
He compared me to other girls
He criticized me to his friends
He said I was insecure and controlling
He picked another female over me
He blamed me for his bad behavior
He didn't protect me
He never loved me

I ignored all of it
And I never will again

Lesson 112

Everyone pray for his new girlfriend

She will never know the real him
Because you made him realize
His faults and flaws

And now he's a better liar

Lesson 113

There is a difference between
Loving someone
And
Being in love

Lesson 114

Both of you have to bring
100% for the other

Relationships are not 50/50
They are 100/100

Lesson 115

If you have to ask them if they like you
They probably don't …

Thank you, next

Lesson 116

The red flags
Will always come back
To haunt you

Address them now
So it doesn't bite you in the a** later

Lesson 117

Stop focusing on fixing a man
Focus on fixing yourself

Lesson 118

The 5 C's of Love:

Commitment
Communication
Compassion
Comprehension
Compromise

Lesson 119

If he's not solving your problems
He's adding to them

Lesson 120

I hate the number 2
Why?
Because you always made me feel like
I was your 2nd choice

Be with someone
Who treats you as number 1

Lesson 121

If he treats you badly
Because you are ahead of him
Leave

If he doesn't respect
Your boundaries
Leave

If he isn't kind
And has no morals
Leave

Lesson 122

You don't have to forget them
You just have to realize
They are not the same person
They used to be

Lesson 123

There are fights in all relationships
Don't give up so quickly
Over a small argument

Sometimes you aren't toxic
You are just young and in love

Lesson 124

Stalking his page
On your burner account
Is delaying your healing

Lesson 125

Keep your relationship private
Other people love to ruin good things

Lesson 126

I would've chosen you
In every lifetime
But you couldn't even choose me
In this one

Lesson 127

Sometimes
Love isn't enough
You can love someone
With every bone in your body
And still know
They aren't the one for you

Lesson 128

If you have someone
Who will do anything to make you happy
Hold onto them

People don't realize
That love doesn't come so easily
Until it's gone

Part 3

Life

Lesson 129

Don't let anyone's words
Change your perception of yourself
The right people will never put you down

Lesson 130

Sometimes what holds us back from learning
Are things we previously picked up
And hold onto as true

Lesson 131

If you focus on the hurt
You will continue to suffer

If you focus on the lesson
You will continue to grow

Lesson 132

You have to be morally rich to truly appreciate
Being financially rich

Lesson 133

No one likes a narcissist
Keep a humble heart

Lesson 134

Stop using failure as an excuse
To not go after your dreams

Lesson 135

You can't get what you want
When you don't know what you want

And sometimes

Knowing what you want comes from
Getting what you don't want first

Lesson 136

Compliments from women
Are way more meaningful and fulfilling
Than compliments from men

Lesson 137

You will outgrow people
And that's ok

Lesson 138

Failure only becomes failure
When you choose to sit down
And not get back up

Lesson 139

You can't move forward
If you keep looking in the rearview mirror

Lesson 140

Someone who overthinks
Is also someone
Who overloves

Lesson 141

Make time to see your family
Money comes back around
But time runs out

Lesson 142

People come into your life
As either a lesson
Or a lifetime

Lesson 143

People are nothing thinking about you
Good or bad
As much as you think they are

Lesson 144

Whatever you are currently feeling
Will pass

I promise

Lesson 145

Say yes to every invite
Even if it's not your favorite activity

Lesson 146

Take your Vitamin D
Especially
During those short winter days

Lesson 147

Your 20's is the time
To work on loving yourself first
Before loving someone else

Understanding things like:
What your boundaries are
How you want to be treated
Knowing your self-worth
Discovering your career
Making time for your friends
Thinking financially

Lesson 148

Don't change who you are
To fit someone's mold
Of what is desirable

Lesson 149

Time doesn't heal all wounds
You have to do the work
Along with time

Or you will stay stuck where you are
Indefinitely

Lesson 150

Give yourself a break
Give yourself time
Give yourself a second chance
Give yourself credit
Give yourself confidence
Give yourself energy
Give yourself kindness
Give yourself love

Lesson 151

The truth will always come out

Lesson 152

Despite whatever pressure you feel
There is no timeline
And no boxes to checkoff

Live at your own pace

Lesson 153

Being nice is FREE
Choose kindness, seriously

Lesson 154

No one knows what they're doing
They just act like they do

Lesson 155

Comparison is the thief of joy
There is always something
Prettier
Shinier
Smarter
Faster
Stronger

Learn to be satisfied
With yourself

Lesson 156

Stop seeking validation from others
And learn to be secure
In your ownself

Lesson 157

The things people do and say
Has to do more with them
Than with you

Don't take it personally

Lesson 158

Vaping is worse than cigarettes
Chew some gum

Lesson 159

The key to healing
Is knowing your self worth

Lesson 160

It's ok to be delusional
Delusional will take you much further
Than reality

Lesson 161

If it costs you your peace
It's wayyyy too expensive

Lesson 162

Manipulation is when they focus on
How you reacted instead of
How they treated you

Lesson 163

Are you doing things for yourself
Or for other people?

Lesson 164

If it brings you happiness
It's productive

Lesson 165

Respect > History

Lesson 166

Everyone will disappoint you
At some point

It's inevitable
Because we are human

Don't be surprised when it happens

Lesson 167

You are allowed
To change your mind

Lesson 168

You can't make yourself happy
While bringing misery
To other people

Lesson 169

Save and invest as early as possible

Lesson 170

Work hard today so tomorrow can be easier

Lesson 171

You can be working hard
But still be depressed

You can be surrounded by friends
But still feel lonely

You can make progress
But still feel the trauma

You can be super confident
But still have anxiety

Be kind to yourself and others
We are all fighting our own battles

Lesson 172

It is never too late
To reinvent yourself

Your past does not have to
Equal your future unless
You choose to live there

Lesson 173

I wish I could tell my teenage self
That my real soulmate
Is me

Lesson 174

Your self-love
Has to be stronger
Than your desire
To be loved

Lesson 175

They are watching, regardless
They are talking, regardless

So do you, regardless

Lesson 176

The day you plant the seed
Is not the same day you eat the fruit

Healing takes time

Lesson 177

Not everyone will appreciate you
Because they are too busy
Battling their own insecurities

Lesson 178

People cannot become
Who they want to become
Because they are too attached
To who they used to be

If your past self didn't work for you
Why are you stuck in the past?

Lesson 179

People may judge you because
They don't have what you have

Lesson 180

When life wants you to make a change
You will feel
So sad, lost, depressed
That you will be forced
To finally make that change

Lesson 181

The easiest thing to do
Is to complain
The most difficult task
Is to work on your dreams

Lesson 182

Don't promise when you're
Happy
Don't reply when you're
Angry
Don't decide when you're
Sad

Lesson 183

Sometimes
People won't invite you places
Because
You are bright
You standout
You are the center of attention

And it's too much for them

Lesson 184

You will be the happiest person
Once you start enjoying
The progress of your life
Instead of the destination

Lesson 185

Never let your happiness depend on anyone

Lesson 186

I am not responsible
For what is done to me

But
I am responsible
For my emotional reaction

Lesson 187

Trust is EARNED
It is to NOT be given freely

Lesson 188

The best revenge is becoming
The best version of yourself

Lesson 189

The relationships in my life
Are mirrors of the relationship
I have with myself

Lesson 190

There is always conflict in life
But you must learn how to deal with it
While still enjoying life

Lesson 191

If it feels off
It probably is

Lesson 192

The universe always has
Three answers:

Yes
Not yet
I have something better

Lesson 193

You shouldn't have to beg
For anything
You know you deserve

Read that again

Lesson 194

Focus on yourself
Focus on your goals
Focus on your happiness
Focus on loving yourself first
Focus on maintaining your peace

Lesson 195

Be mindful of who you vent to

Lesson 196

Small steps
Every day
Will add up

Lesson 197

Be thankful
For difficult people in your life
Because they have shown you
Who you don't want to be

Lesson 198

You will regret
The things you didn't try to do
Way more than
The things you tried and failed

Lesson 199

Instead of
Why is this happening to me?
Think
What am I supposed to learn
From this?

Lesson 200

In your 20's
Everything feels like the end of the world
But it's not

It's just the beginning

*I am thankful for these experiences
and I hope these lessons
will guide you in the right direction*

Printed in Great Britain
by Amazon